# Practice Papers for SQA Exams

## Standard Grade | Credit

# French

ISBN 978-1-84372-769-9

Published by
Leckie & Leckie Ltd, 4 Queen Street, Edinburgh, EH2 1JE
Tel: 0131 220 6831 Fax: 0131 225 9987
enquiries@leckieandleckie.co.uk   www.leckieandleckie.co.uk

A CIP Catalogue record for this book is available from the British Library.

Leckie & Leckie Ltd is a division of Huveaux plc.

Questions and answers in this book do not emanate from SQA. All of our entirely new and original Practice
Papers have been written by experienced authors working directly for the publisher.

# Introduction

## Layout of the Book

This book contains practice exam papers, which mirror the actual SQA exam as much as possible. The layout, paper colour and question level are all similar to the actual exam that you will sit, so that you are familiar with what the exam paper will look like. The CD contains three practice listening exams.

The answer section is at the back of the book. Each answer contains a worked out answer or solution so that you can see how the right answer has been arrived at. The answers also include practical tips on how to tackle certain types of questions, details of how marks are awarded and advice on just what the examiners will be looking for.

Revision advice is provided in this introductory section of the book, so please read on!

## How To Use This Book

The Practice Papers can be used in two main ways:

1. You can complete an entire practice paper as preparation for the final exam. If you would like to use the book in this way, you can either complete the practice paper under exam style conditions by setting yourself a time for each paper and answering it as well as possible without using any references or notes. Alternatively, you can answer the practice paper questions as a revision exercise, using your notes to produce a model answer. Your teacher may mark these for you.

2. You can use the Topic Index at the front of this book to find all the questions within the book that deal with a specific topic. This allows you to focus specifically on areas that you particularly want to revise or, if you are mid-way through your course, it lets you practise answering exam-style questions for just those topics that you have studied.

## Revision Advice

Work out a revision timetable for each week's work in advance – remember to cover all of your subjects and to leave time for homework and breaks. For example:

| Day | 6pm–6.45pm | 7pm–8pm | 8.15pm–9pm | 9.15pm–10pm |
|---|---|---|---|---|
| Monday | Homework | Homework | English revision | Chemistry revision |
| Tuesday | Maths revision | Physics revision | Homework | Free |
| Wednesday | Geography revision | Modern Studies revision | English revision | French revision |
| Thursday | Homework | Maths revision | Chemistry revision | Free |
| Friday | Geography revision | French revision | Free | Free |
| Saturday | Free | Free | Free | Free |
| Sunday | Modern Studies revision | Maths revision | Modern Studies revision | Homework |

Make sure that you have at least one evening free a week to relax, socialise and re-charge your batteries. It also gives your brain a chance to process the information that you have been feeding it all week.

Arrange your study time into one hour or 30 minutes sessions, with a break between sessions e.g. 6pm – 7pm, 7.15pm–7.45pm, 8pm–9pm. Try to start studying as early as possible in the evening when your brain is still alert and be aware that the longer you put off starting, the harder it will be to start!

Study a different subject in each session, except for the day before an exam.

Do something different during your breaks between study sessions – have a cup of tea, or listen to some music. Don't let your 15 minutes expanded into 20 or 25 minutes though!

Have your class notes and any textbooks available for your revision to hand as well as plenty of blank paper, a pen, etc.

## In the Exam

Watch your time and pace yourself carefully. Work out roughly how much time you can spend on each answer and try to stick to this.

Be clear before the exam what the instructions are likely to be e.g. how many questions you should answer in each section. The practice papers will help you to become familiar with the exam's instructions.

Read the question thoroughly before you begin to answer it – make sure you know exactly what the question is asking you to do. If the question is in sections e.g. 15a, 15b, 15c, etc., make sure that you can answer each section before you start writing.

Plan your answer by jotting down keywords, a mindmap or reminders of the important things to include in your answer. Cross them off as you deal with them and check them before you move on to the next question to make sure that you haven't forgotten anything.

Don't repeat yourself as you will not get any more marks for saying the same thing twice. This also applies to annotated diagrams which will not get you any extra marks if the information is repeated in the written part of your answer.

Give proper explanations. A common error is to give descriptions rather than explanations. If you are asked to explain something, you should be giving reasons. Check your answer to an 'explain' question and make sure that you have used plenty of linking words and phrases such as 'because', 'this means that', 'therefore', 'so', 'so that', 'due to', 'since' and 'the reason is'.

Use the resources provided. Some questions will ask you to 'describe and explain' and provide an example or a case study for you to work from. Make sure that you take any relevant data from these resources.

Good luck!

# Topic Index

| Topic | Exam A (Reading) | Exam B (Reading) | Exam C (Reading) | Exam A (Listening) | Exam B (Listening) | Exam C (Listening) |
|---|---|---|---|---|---|---|
| Family Relationships (parents) | | 1 | | 9 | 2, 3, 4 | |
| Family Relationships (siblings) | | | | 2 | | |
| Upbringing/ Background | | | | 1, 2, 3, 4 | | 6 |
| Daily Routine | | | | 8 | 3, 4 | |
| Social Arrangements | | | | | 1, 10 | 11, 12 |
| Social Interaction | | | | | | 2, 10 |
| Social Issues | 3, 5 | | 4, 5 | | | |
| Environment | | 2 | | | | |
| Education (pupils) | 1, 2 | 4 | | | | 1 |
| Education (schools) | 3 | 4 | | 5 | 1 | |
| Education (past) | | | | | | 8 |
| Education (future) | | | | 10 | | 9 |
| Health and Illness | 4, 5 | | | 8 | | 1, 10 |
| Sport | | 1, 2 | | | 10, 11, 12 | |
| Free Time and Entertainment | 2 | | 3, 4, 5 | | | 12 |
| Jobs (general) | | | | 1 | | 7 |
| Jobs (future) | | | | 11 | 6 | |
| Food and Drink (customs) | | | | 6, 7 | 9 | |
| Communications and IT | 6 | | 2 | 13 | | |
| Holidays (past) | | | | | 7 | 1, 3, 4 |
| Holidays (future) | 6 | | | | 5 | |
| Travel and Transport | 4 | | | | | 1 |

# Topic Index

| | Exam A (Reading) | Exam B (Reading) | Exam C (Reading) | Exam A (Listening) | Exam B (Listening) | Exam C (Listening) |
|---|---|---|---|---|---|---|

# French

## Standard Grade: Credit

Practice Papers
For SQA Exams

**Exam A**
**Credit Level**
**Reading**

**Fill in these boxes:**

Name of centre

Town

Forename(s)

Surname

Make sure you read the questions carefully.

You have 1 hour to complete this paper.

Try to answer all of the questions in the time allowed. Remember to answer in English.

Write your answers in the spaces provided.

Make sure you write as neatly as you can and answer in sentences wherever possible.

You can use a French dictionary.

Leckie×Leckie

Scotland's leading educational publishers

1. François Bégaudeau's best-selling novel 'Entre les murs' tells the story of his experiences as a teacher in a *collège* in the outskirts of Paris.

It was made into a film in 2006, directed by Laurent Cantet, in which François Bégaudeau himself plays the part of the teacher.

While surfing the internet, you come across this extract of an interview with the French film magazine, *Actualité Cinéma*, where the director explains the kind of teacher that François Bégaudeau is :-

---

***Entre les murs***
*un film de Laurent Cantet*

**Interview**

Actualité Cinéma : Quel enseignant est François?

Laurent Cantet : Eh bien, François a compris que pour communiquer quelque chose à ses élèves il faut d'abord les captiver. Si on veut communiquer, il faut avoir des rapports très directs avec ses élèves. Etre prof, c'est s'impliquer totalement, ne pas seulement avoir un savoir mais aimer également le dialogue. Si François est un bon professeur, c'est parce qu'il adore la discussion. Les professeurs sont des comédiens, ils ont l'habitude d'improviser.

$$2 + 2 = 4$$
$$2 \times 2 = 4$$

---

(a) According to the film director, Laurent Cantet, what did the writer François Bégaudeau understand was necessary in order to communicate properly with pupils? Mention two things.

_____

_____

(2)

(b) What aspect of François' teaching style does Laurent Cantet clearly admire?

_____

_____

(1)

(c) How does Laurent Cantet define teachers? Mention two things.

_____

_____

(2)

**2.** The film features real pupils in a real school in Paris. The director explains why :-

> Laurent Cantet : Ce qui m'intéressait c'était de réaliser une fiction
> documentée, qui écoute, qui regarde réellement ce qui se passe dans un vrai
> collège. Je n'ai pas vu énormément de films qui décrivent le quotidien d'une
> école comme on a essayé de le faire. C'est les élèves qui ont joué et rejoué
> les scènes, qui ont crée des personnages. François a dit aux élèves de ne pas
> changer leur langage réel : 'C'est très bien de parler commes vous le faites'
> a-t-il dit.

(a) Describe the kind of film that the director, Laurent Cantet, wished to make.
Mention two things.

_____

_____

_____

(2)

(b) What specific advice did the author, François, give to the pupils during the
filming of his book?

_____

_____

(1)

**3.** The choice of school was important to both the director and the author, as Laurent Cantet goes on to explain in his magazine interview :-

> Laurent Cantet: Oui, alors, le choix du collège a été pour nous tous quelque chose de très important…on a choisi d'abord le *quartier* à cause de sa vraie mixité d'origine géographique et sociale. Le collège Dalto se trouve effectivement dans ce genre de quartier, c'est l'établissement de banlieue par excellence dans le sens qu'il y une quarantaine de nationalités, qu'on y voit les élèves dont plusieurs sont en bas de l'échelle sociale.

(*a*) Explain why the choice of *area* was so important.

_____

_____

(1)

(*b*) In what sense exactly did the Collège Dalto fit the image of what the film-makers were looking for? Mention two things.

_____

_____

(2)

**4.** Before logging off, your attention is caught by a news flash on 'Actualités', which tells of the death of a French tourist returning from a holiday in central Africa, where he had picked up a rare disease.

---

### *Jeune Français meurt d'une maladie rare après des vacances en Afrique*

Jeudi, vingt-trois heures à l'aéroport de Charles de Gaulle à Paris, et grande panique parmi le service des urgences après l'atterrissage forcé du vol AF 326 du Congo. D'après le porte-parole d'Air France le jeune passager est tombé grièvement malade peu après le décollage : 'Monsieur Giraud se sentait malade pendant la nuit, avait de la fièvre, se plaignait du vertige et a très vite perdu connaissance. Une fois qu'on a atterri on l'a transporté

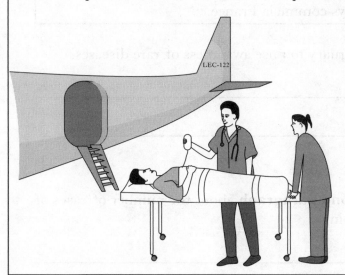

d'urgence à l'hôpital, mais malheureusement il est mort peu après'. Richard Giraud, 21 ans, étudiant de sciences naturelles à la faculté de Lyon, depuis le début de l'année, était parti en Afrique avec sa fiancée, Juliette Jardin, 20 ans, et un nombre d'étudiants de la Communauté Européenne, pour faire du travail bénévole dans un orphelinat au Congo.

---

(*a*) What action did the pilot take to try to save the life of one of his passengers?

_____

(1)

(*b*) According to the Air France spokesman, what were the symptoms of the passenger in question? Mention any three things.

_____

_____

_____

(3)

(*c*) Explain what Richard Giraud had been doing in the Congo?

_____

_____

(2)

**5.** Later on you read an article in a French magazine about rare diseases.

---

### Maladies rares : 3 millions de Français touchés

Plus de 3 millions de patients sont concernés par la Journée Internationale des Maladies Rares, qui se déroule en France le 28 février.

Pour être rares, ces maladies à faible prévalence sont nombreuses : il en existerait plus de 5,500, mais ce chiffre évolue sans arrêt. D'après le site *Orphanet*, deux nouvelles maladies rares sont décrites chaque mois dans la littérature scientifique.

Une maladie est dite rare lorsqu'elle touche moins d'une personne sur 200. Soit moins de 30,000 dans un pays comme la France.

---

(*a*) What is being held on 28 February to raise awareness of rare diseases?

_____

_____

(1)

(*b*) What are we told **in the second paragraph** about the number of cases of rare diseases? Mention two things.

_____

_____

(2)

(*c*) What fact concerning rare diseases has the website *Orphanet* recently published?

_____

_____

(2)

(*d*) What definition of 'rare disease' is offered at the end of the article?

_____

_____

(1)

**6.** Later, you receive a card from your French pen friend inviting you over to France this summer.

Lens, 26 mars

Salut!

Juste un petit mot avant de partir avec l'échange scolaire en Allemagne pour te demander si tu serais libre pour nous rejoindre en Bretagne cet été. Nous espérons passer une quinzaine (début juillet) chez mes cousins sur la côte où on pourrait faire plein de choses qui t'intéresseraient, comme des excursions en bâteau, des randonnées à pied – il y a même un centre de tir à l'arc pas loin de chez eux...

Si cela t'intéresse, écris-moi vite pour qu'on puisse en parler. Je serai là jusqu'à vendredi soir, et après ça en route pour l'Allemagne.

A bientôt j'espère!

**Luc**

(a) Mention any two activities Luc thinks would interest you about the holiday in Brittany.

_____

_____

(2)

(b) Explain why Luc wants you to reply *quickly*.

_____

_____

(1)

**(26)**

[End of question paper]

# French      Standard Grade: Credit

| | |
|---|---|
| Practice Papers<br>For SQA Exams | **Exam A**<br>**Credit Level**<br>**Listening Transcript** |

The listening transcript accompanies the audio CD provided with the book.

Remember that listening transcripts will **not** be provided when you sit your final exam. They are printed here as an additional item to help you with your revision for the listening exam.

Leckie×Leckie
Scotland's leading educational publishers

## Transcript – Practice Exam A

**(t)** You are on holiday in France. You meet a young girl called Clémentine.

**Tu passes des vacances en France. Tu fais la connaissance d'une jeune Française qui s'appelle Clémentine.**

**(t) Question number one**

She tells you a little about her early life. What does she say? Mention any **two** things.

**(f) Moi, je suis née en Tunisie, où j'ai passé les onze premières années de ma vie, car ma mère y travaillait comme médecin à l'hôpital de Tunis, la ville capitale, et mon père était professeur au lycée français là-bas.**

40 seconds

**(t) Question number two**

Clémentine talks about her sisters. What does she say about them? Mention any **one** thing.

**(f) Je suis l'aînée de la famille. Mes deux soeurs sont jumelles et elles sont moins âgées que moi de trois ans.**

40 seconds

**(t) Question number three**

When her family returned to France, Clémentine experienced certain difficulties at first. What exactly did she find difficult? Mention **two** things.

**(f) Lorsqu'on est retourné en France en mille neuf cent quatre-vingt-neuf, j'ai eu du mal à m'adapter à la nouvelle vie. Bien sûr, le climat nord-africain me manquait, mais en plus je trouvais difficile de me faire des amies au début parce que je ne connaissais personne au collège dans notre quartier.**

40 seconds

**(t) Question number four**

Clémentine explains how soon she began to appreciate certain aspects of living there. What did she like best about France? Mention **one** thing. What did her sisters particularly enjoy in their new life? Mention **one** thing.

**(f) Cependant, après quelques mois ici, je me suis fait de très bonnes amies avec lesquelles je passais les grandes vacances tous les ans à faire du camping – soit au bord de la mer sur la côte mediterranéenne, soit dans les bois et les forêts du nord, ou au pied des montagnes à la frontière espagnole. Ce que j'aimais le plus c'était la grande diversité géographique du pays. Quant à mes soeurs, Amélie et Jacqueline, elles étaient membres de l'équipe de gymnastique régionale et pratiquaient ce sport à très haut niveau. Et ça elles appréciaient énormément.**

40 seconds

**(t) Question number five**

Clémentine tells you that Amélie recently spent a year abroad as a pupil. What, does she say, were the benefits of this experience? Mention **two** things.

**(f) Ma soeur, Amélie, vient de passer une année scolaire aux Etats-Unis dans une école américaine afin de perfectionner son anglais. Cela s'est très bien passé et elle parle la langue couramment maintenant. Je crois qu'elle a mûri aussi durant cette expérience inoubliable.**

40 seconds

**(t) Question number six**

Clémentine relates her sister's experiences of American eating habits. What does she say about this? Mention one thing. What, according to her, are the consequences of the eating habits in the United States? Mention **one** thing.

**(f) Amélie a trouvé qu'ils mangent assez mal aux Etats-Unis, par exemple ils vont deux ou trois fois par semaine au fastfood, même parfois au petit déjeuner. Evidemment on risque d'avoir des problèmes de santé à l'avenir, surtout avec l'obésité.**

40 seconds

**(t) Question number seven**

She asks you about the differences in Scottish and French eating habits. What **two** differences in eating habits do you mention? What else do you say?

**(m) Il est vrai que nous mangeons d'habitude plus de sucreries chez nous et pas mal de matières grasses par rapports aux Français. Mais d'autre part je trouve qu'on exagère un peu les différences entres les coutumes culinaires de nos pays. Nous avons fait des progrès dans ce domaine, tu sais!**

40 seconds

**(t) Question number eight**

You ask Clémentine what she does to keep healthy. **Complete** the sentences.

**(f) Ce que je fais, moi, pour rester en bonne santé? Eh bien, il y a un an, ma mère et moi nous nous sommes décidées à aller au gymnase tous les vendredis après l'école, mais finalement faire de l'exercise comme ça c'était tellement pénible qu'on n'y allait pas trop souvent. Mais nous mangeons équilibré et sortons le soir pendant une bonne heure pour nous promener avec le chien à la campagne tout près. A mon avis, c'est la meilleure façon de rester en pleine forme.**

40 seconds

**(t) Question number nine**

You ask her about how she gets on with her mother. Why, according to Clémentine, do they generally get on well? Mention **one** thing. What does her mother sometimes forget, however? Mention **one** thing.

**(f) Dans l'ensemble, on s'entend assez bien, car elle me traîte comme une adulte, mais il faut avouer que de temps en temps elle est trop protectrice et parfois elle oublie qu'à mon âge j'ai besoin d'un peu plus de liberté.**

40 seconds

**(t) Question number ten**

Clémentine then goes on to talk of her future plans. What might she study? Mention **one** thing. What change will this new life offer her? Mention **one** thing.

**(f) Après l'année de terminale au lycée, j'espère aller à la faculté à Montpellier afin de poursuivre des études de droit ou bien de langues vivantes. Je compte y trouver une chambre en ville ce qui m'obligerait a être plus indépendante.**

40 seconds

**(t) Question number eleven**

She considers her future career possibilities. What reasons does she give for not wanting to follow in her father's footsteps? Mention any **three** things.

**(f) En ce qui concerne un métier, je n'ai pas en ce moment d'idée fixe. Mais devenir professeur comme mon père ne me dit rien car si je pense à lui qui est prof depuis une trentaine d'années, c'est un boulot vraiment exigeant avec toutes ces heures supplémentaires qu'on doit faire à préparer ses cours, corriger ses copies, s'engager dans les activités parascolaires et assister aux réunions. Je t'assure que ce n'est pas pour moi, cette vie!**

40 seconds

**(t) Question number twelve**

Clémentine explains what is important to her in a job. What does she say? Mention **one** thing.

**(f) L'important, selon moi, c'est de trouver un métier où l'on se sent vraiment utile, où je pourrais aider les autres. Etre bien rémunérée ou avoir de longues vacances, cela n'a aucune importance pour moi.**

40 seconds

**(t) Question number thirteen**

At the end of your stay in France, Clémentine asks you to stay in touch. What suggestion does she make about this?. Mention **one** thing.

**(f) Alors, je te souhaite bon retour en Ecosse. Et si tu as envie de rester en contact, ça me plairait beaucoup. Puisque j'ai des problèmes avec mon ordinateur actuellement je te passe mon numéro de portable, d'accord?**

40 seconds

**(t) End of test.**

**Now check your answers.**

[End of transcript]

# French

# Standard Grade: Credit

| Practice Papers<br>For SQA Exams | Time allowed:<br>30 Minutes (approx) | **Exam A**<br>**Credit Level**<br>**Listening** |
|---|---|---|

**Fill in these boxes:**

Name of centre

Town

Forename(s)

Surname

The listening exam should take approximately 30 minutes.

You will hear a number of items in French. These items are repeated three times.

There will then be a pause to let you write your answer. Make sure you read the questions carefully.

Remember to answer in English and write your answers in the spaces provided.

You cannot use a French dictionary.

You are on holiday in France. You meet a young girl called Clémentine.

Tu passes des vacances en France. Tu fais la connaissance d'une jeune Française qui s'appelle Clémentine.

1. She tells you a little about her early life. What does she say? Mention any two things.

_____

_____

(2)

2. Clémentine talks about her sisters. What does she say about them? Mention any one thing.

_____

_____

(1)

3. When her family returned to France, Clémentine experienced certain difficulties at first. What were they? Mention any two things.

_____

_____

(2)

4. Clementine explains how soon she began to appreciate certain aspects of living there.

(a) What did she like best about living in France?

_____

_____

(1)

(b) Which leisure activity did her sisters particularly enjoy here?

_____

_____

(1)

**5.** Clémentine tells you that her sister, Amélie, recently spent a year abroad in an American school as a pupil. What does she think were the benefits of this experience? Mention two things.

_____

_____

(2)

**6.** Clémentine relates Amélie's experience of American eating habits.

    (*a*) What does she say about this? Mention any one thing.

_____

_____

(1)

    (*b*) What is the consequence of these eating habits? Mention any one thing.

_____

_____

(1)

**7.** Clémentine asks you about the differences between Scottish and French eating habits.

    (*a*) What two differences do you mention?

_____

_____

(2)

    (*b*) What else do you say? Mention any one thing.

_____

_____

(1)

**8.** You ask Clémentine what she does to keep healthy. Complete the sentences :

Every Friday

_____

but that kind of physical exercise

_____

Now they eat

_____

and in the evening

_____

_____

(2)

9. You ask her how she gets on with her mother.

(a) Why do they generally get on well? Mention one thing.

_____

_____

(1)

(b) What does her mother sometimes forget, however? Mention one thing.

_____

_____

(1)

10. Clémentine talks of her future plans.

(a) What will she study at university?

_____

_____

(1)

(b) What change will this new life offer her? Mention any one thing.

_____

(1)

11. She considers her future career possibilities. For what reasons does she not want to follow in her father's footsteps? Mention any three things.

_____

_____

_____

(3)

12. Clémentine explains what is important to her in a job. What does she say? Mention any one thing.

_____

_____

(1)

13. At the end of your stay in France, Clémentine asks you to stay in touch. What suggestion does she make about this?

_____

_____

(1)

TOTAL (25)

[End of question paper]

# French

# Standard Grade: Credit

| Practice Papers | Time allowed: | **Exam B** |
| For SQA Exams | 1hour | **Credit Level** |
| | | **Reading** |

**Fill in these boxes:**

Name of centre

Town

Forename(s)

Surname

Make sure you read the questions carefully.

You have 1 hour to complete this paper.

Try to answer all of the questions in the time allowed. Remember to answer in English.

Write your answers in the spaces provided.

Make sure you write as neatly as you can and answer in sentences wherever possible.

You can use a French dictionary.

Leckie × Leckie

Scotland's leading educational publishers

**1.** You come across an article in a French magazine called *Sport et Santé* which lists the top three sports for fitness.

| sport | À quel âge commencer? | caractéristiques |
|---|---|---|
| La natation | La brasse : 4/5 ans<br>le crawl : 7/8 ans | C'est un sport complet où tous les muscles doivent travailler sans risque de blessures.<br><br>C'est un bon sport pour les asthmatiques ainsi que pour les diabétiques. Les enfants handicappés en profitent énormément car ce sport leur permet de prendre de l'exercise individuellement en présence d'un surveillant de baignade. |
| L'équitation | Poney : à partir de 5/6 ans<br><br>Cheval : à partir de 12/13 ans | Bien que cette activité sportive soit exigeante, les muscles ne travaillent pas excessivement pourvu qu'on ne perde pas l'équilibre.<br><br>On a l'occasion de travailler harmonieusement avec l'animal tout en profitant de la vie en plein air. |
| Le football | Pour tous les âges, mais compétition à partir de 11/12 ans seulement | Ce sport simple et collectif facilite les relations avec les autres en développant la coordination des mouvements.<br><br>Ce sport de l'équipe complet est pratiqué par 15% de ceux qui ont plus de 40 ans. |

For each of the three sports, complete the sentences below.

Swimming is a complete sport where

_____

Handicapped children benefit from swimming because

_____

Horse riding will not overwork your muscles provided

_____

When riding you have the opportunity to

_____

Football encourages _____

_____

(5)

2. Later in the same magazine you read an article in which the French rugby star, Sébastien Chabal, talks about his sport :

> **Sebastien Chabal parle à *'Sport et Santé'* ...**
>
> *'Sport et Santé* : Sébastien Chabal, après votre longue tournée avec l'équipe nationale de France en Nouvelle-Zélande, avez-vous toujours faim sous le maillot des Bleus?*
>
> *Chabal* : Oui, absolument! J'attends mon premier match, contre les Ecossais, avec impatience. J'adore jouer en Ecosse, car il y a une bonne ambiance chez eux et on joue avec passion...*
>
> *'Sport et Santé'* : Qu'est-ce qui vous inspire? D'où vient la motivation après une longue saison?*
>
> *Chabal* : Nous sommes là pour représenter notre pays, faire au mieux. Le rugby reste avant tout une question de collectif, plus que d'indivualités, et c'est ça que j'aime. Etre membre d'une équipe c'est comme se retrouver dans une grande famille.*

(a) What does the interviewer ask in the first question?

_____

_____

(1)

(b) Chabal clearly enjoys playing in Scotland. What does he say? Mention two things.

_____

_____

(2)

(c) As an international rugby player, what is he motivated by? Mention any two things.

_____

_____

(1)

(d) What does Chabal compare playing this team game to?

_____

(1)

**3.** Later on that week you receive an email from your pen friend, Philippe, in France where he describes a project he is working on to raise awareness about the need to protect the environment in his area.

---

Bonjour!

Je t'écris pour t'expliquer le projet 'vert' qu'on fait en classe actuellement depuis quelques semaines. Notre objectif était de rechercher ce qu'on fait pour protéger la nature ici en Normandie. Tout d'abord, le prof d'histoire-géo nous a obligé d'écrire aux ministres et aux industries de fabrication pour leur demander ce qu'ils font pour l'environnement, et la plupart d'entre eux ont répondu. Voici un résumé de leurs réponses :-

d)  Nous encourageons les gens à acheter seulement les produits 'verts', c'est-à-dire ceux qui ne sont pas testés sur les animaux et qui ne contiennent pas de chimiques nuisibles à l'environnement.

di)  Nous avons également ouvert des centres de recyclage dans une trentaine d'endroits où on peut recycler les ordures telles que les bouteilles vides et les vieux papiers.

dii)  Notre campagne 'Sauvez la terre' a réussi à interdire la construction de plusieurs hypermarchés et usines dans les espaces verts en Normandie – des espaces protégés à cause de leur beauté, de leur flore et de leur faune

Je ne sais pas si ça t'intéresse, mais je t'envoie aussi l'article dans notre revue scolaire sur l'échange! Tu trouveras quelques commentaires intéressants là-dedans!

A bientôt,

Philippe

---

(*a*)  What was the purpose of the project on the environment?

_____

_____

(1)

(*b*)  Which **two** groups did the pupils write to?

_____

_____

(1)

(*c*)  Define the 'green products' that environmentalists are keen to promote. Mention any one thing.

_____

_____

(2)

(*d*) What did the campaign 'Sauvez la terre' succeed in preventing?

_____

_____

(1)

(*e*) Why was this important?

_____

_____

(1)

**4.** The attachment is an article which contains some pupil comments on the experience of the exchange with your school earlier on in the year.

Ghislaine, 14 ans

J'ai trouvé l'expérience vraiment éducative – de voir un peu les différences pédagogiques, les moyens d'enseigner et d'apprendre en classe. Surtout l'idée de faire tant d'activités en groupe, au lieu de travailler tout le temps individuellement, m'a beaucoup impressionnée.

Ludovic, 13 ans

Malheureusement, je ne me suis pas très bien entendu avec mon partenaire écossais, malgré les efforts de sa famille. Il ne partageait pas mes intérêts et ne s'intéressait qu'à jouer sur l'ordinateur, ce qui n'est pas mon truc.

Benjamin, 14 ans

Ce qui m'a frappé le plus, c'était les coutumes culinaires – en Ecosse on mangeait rarement ensemble à table. Chacun prenait ce qu'il voulait à l'heure qui convenait, et on grignotait sans cesse des sucreries entre les repas. Il faut dire que leur régime n'est pas très bon pour la santé, en règle général, bien que (je l'avoue!) j'adore le poisson frites!

Nathalie, 14 ans

Quel séjour splendide en Ecosse! On a vraiment tout fait pour me mettre à l'aise et pour me donner un excellent souvenir du pays. J'aimerais y retourner et en fait je viens de recevoir une invitation à passer une quinzaine cet été chez la famille écossaise! On ira sans aucun doute rendre visite aux grandparents qui habitent dans le nord-ouest. Chouette!

(a) What really struck Ghislaine as different about the classroom experience in Scotland? Mention any one thing.

_____

_____

(1)

(b) Why did Ludovic not get on with his partner? Mention two things.

_____

_____

(2)

(c) What are the Scottish eating habits, according to Benjamin? Mention any three things.

_____

_____

_____

(3)

(d) Nathalie clearly enjoyed her stay in Scotland. Why? Mention any one thing.

_____

_____

(1)

(e) What has she just received an invitation to do? Mention two things.

_____

_____

_____

(2)

Total (26)

[End of question paper]

# French

## Standard Grade: Credit

Practice Papers
For SQA Exams

**Exam B**
**Credit Level**
**Listening Transcript**

The listening transcript accompanies the audio CD provided with the book.

Remember that listening transcripts will **not** be provided when you sit your final exam. They are printed here as an additional item to help you with your revision for the listening exam.

Leckie × Leckie
Scotland's leading educational publishers

**Transcript – Credit Level**

**(t)** **You are spending a week in France with your school exchange partner, Bazire (m).**

Tu passes une semaine en France chez ton correspondant.

40 seconds

**(t)** **Question number one**

Bazire says you will be going to the tennis club after school with friends. What does he say about the tennis club? Complete the sentences.

**(m)** **Ce soir, on va au club de tennis avec des amis du lycée. Le jeudi il y a toujours beaucoup de monde là-bas, donc on doit arriver avant cinq heures si possible. Sinon on aura du mal à trouver un court de tennis.**

40 seconds

**(t)** **Question number two**

He tells you what his parents normally think about his going out during the week. What does he say? He goes on to explain that things are different just now. What reasons does he give for this? Complete the sentences.

**(m)** **Normalement je n'ai pas le droit de sortir pendant la semaine. Mais vu que c'est la fin du trimestre et qu'on reçoit actuellement le groupe d'élèves écossais, ils sont plus compréhensif que d'habitude.**

40 seconds

**(t)** **Question number three**

Bazire mentions the reasons why his parents are normally reluctant to let him go out on school days. What does he say? Mention two things.

**(m)** **D'abord, ils s'inquiètent un peu parce que j'ai plein de devoirs à faire, et c'est une année très importante au lycée. Et puis il y a des endroits en ville où l'on ne se sent pas en sécurité le soir même si on est avec ses copains.**

40 seconds

**(t)** **Question number four**

Bazire tells you about his relationship with his parents. What does he say about his father? Mention one thing. Why do they sometimes argue? Give one reason.

(m) **Généralement il faut dire que je m'entends assez bien avec mes parents. Mais, en même temps, mon père est beaucoup trop protecteur et ne me laisse jamais faire quoique ce soit seul. Des fois on se dispute au sujet des questions concernant la liberté ou l'indépendance.**

40 seconds

(t) **Question number five**

He explains that he would like to go off on holiday with friends this summer rather than with his parents. What are his plans? Mention one thing. What does his mother think of this idea? Mention one thing.

(m) **J'aimerais partir en vacances cet été au mois de juillet avec mes copains du lycée. Nous voudrions partir faire du camping à la montagne près de la frontière espagnole. Mais ma mère pense que je devrais rester à la maison et trouver un emploi avant de faire des projets de vacances.**

40 seconds

(t) **Question number six**

Bazire hopes to find a job soon so that he can earn some money before the summer holidays. What exactly would the job entail? What will he find difficult?

(m) **Mais moi j'ai l'intention de trouver du travail à mi-temps presque tout de suite. Les parents d'un camarade de classe ont un petit restaurant nord-africain au centre-ville et j'ai de la chance puisqu'ils ont besoin de quelqu'un pour travailler dans la cuisine et de débarrasser les tables à la fin de la soirée le vendredi et le samedi. Donc comme ça j'aurai l'occasion de gagner un peu d'argent qui me permettra de partir l'été. Ce que je trouve difficile, c'est de faire des économies et ne pas dépenser mon argent immédiatement. Il va falloir faire des efforts!**

40 seconds

(t) **Question number seven**

The next day you meet one of Bazire's friends, Thomas, who has just spent a period of time in Scotland. What was he doing there? Mention one thing. Why did he enjoy his stay so much? Mention two things.

(m) **Je viens de passer six mois en Ecosse à la faculté de St-Andrews, avec un groupe d'étudiants dans le cadre du programme Erasmus, qui permet aux étudiants français d'etudier dans des universités à l'étranger. Cela a été une expérience inoubliable, car j'ai pu joindre mes deux passions dans la vie – étudier l'histoire écossaise et jouer au golf!**

40 seconds

(t) **Question number eight**

Thomas tells you about the good and the bad experiences of life as a foreign student. What does he say?

**(m)** Tout le monde a été extrêmement gentil et aimable et les autres étudiants m'ont accueilli très chaleureusement. Pourtant, j'ai trouvé l'accent parfois dur à comprendre, surtout quand on parlait vite dans les magasins ou dans les pubs. Ce n'était pas exactement l'anglais qu'on m'avait appris à l'école!

40 seconds

**(t)** Question number nine

He mentions his experiences of eating in Scotland. What had people warned him of before he left France? Mention one thing. What did he discover? Mention one thing.

**(m)** On m'avait averti avant d'arriver en Ecosse que la nourriture serait tellement mauvaise et malsaine avec beaucoup de matières grasses. Mais au contraire, j'ai très bien mangé et j'étais vraiment étonné par la qualité de la cuisine au réfectoire des étudiants. On dirait que vous avez fait du progrès, les Ecossais!

40 seconds

**(t)** Question number ten

Thomas asks whether you would like to go to the local rugby match at the weekend. Why is it an important match? Mention one thing. What does he say about the local rugby team that he supports? Mention two things.

**(m)** Ça te dirait d'aller voir le match de rugby ce week-end? C'est la demi-finale de la coupe régionale et nous avons en ce moment une équipe très forte, dont deux membres sont sélectionnés pour l'équipe nationale. Je sais que les Ecossais s'intéressent au rugby et quand j'étais en Ecosse je suis allé voir plusieurs rencontres.

40 seconds

**(t)** Question number eleven

Thomas explains that there is quite a number of foreign players in the French Rugby league at present. Mention one good thing about this. Explain what the problem is.

**(m)** En France actuellement il y a pas mal de joueurs qui viennent de différents pays, ce qui fait que le sport devient un spectacle plus passionnant pour tout le monde. Mais, de l'autre côté, ces joueurs anglais ou australiens ou néo-zélandais doivent être bien rémunérés, et donc le prix des tickets a beaucoup augmenté dans les dernières années.

40 seconds

**(t)   Question number twelve**

Thomas goes on to explain that there are some problems communicating with foreign players who do not understand French. What does he say some clubs are doing about this? Mention one thing.

**(m)   Ces joueurs n'ont pas toujours un niveau de français très avancé, et les entraîneurs ne parlent pas forcément anglais, donc quelques clubs insistent que les étrangers prennent des cours particuliers pour améliorer leur français. Tu imagines, les vedettes de rugby dans une salle de classe!**

40 seconds

**(t)   End of test.**

**Now check your answers.**

[End of transcript]

# French      Standard Grade: Credit

Practice Papers
For SQA Exams

**Exam B**
**Credit Level**
**Listening**

---

**Fill in these boxes:**

Name of centre

Town

Forename(s)

Surname

The listening exam should take approximately 30 minutes.

You will hear a number of items in French. These items are repeated three times.

There will then be a pause to let you write your answer. Make sure you read the questions carefully.

Remember to answer in English and write your answers in the spaces provided.

You cannot use a French dictionary.

Leckie×Leckie
Scotland's leading educational publishers

You are spending a week in France with your school exchange partner, Bazire.

Tu passes une semaine en France chez ton correspondant, Bazire.

1. Bazire says you will be going to the tennis club after school with friends. What does he say about the tennis club? Complete the sentences.

   On Thursdays _____

   (1)

   If you arrive after 5 p.m., _____

   _____

   (1)

2. He tells you what his parents think about his going out during the week.

   What does he say? He explains that things are different just now.

   Why is this?

   Complete the sentences.

   Normally, _____

   (1)

   But at present, _____

   _____

   (1)

3. What do Bazire's parents sometimes worry about? Mention two things.

   _____

   _____

   (2)

**4.** Bazire tells you about his relationship with his parents.

    (*a*) What does he say about his father? Mention any one thing.

    _____

                                                                 (1)

    (*b*) Why do they sometimes argue?

    _____

                                                                  (1)

**5.** He explains that he would like to go on holiday with his friends this summer rather than with his parents.

    (*a*) What are his plans?

    _____

                                                                  (1)

    (*b*) What does his mother think of this idea?

    _____

                                                                    (1)

**6.** Bazire hopes to find a part-time job soon.

    (*a*) What would the job entail? Mention any one thing.

    _____

                                                                  (1)

    (*b*) What will he find difficult?

    _____

                                                                    (1)

7.  The next day you meet one of Bazire's friends, Thomas, who has just spent some time in Scotland.

    (a)  What was he doing there?

    _____

    (1)

    (b)  Why did he enjoy his stay so much?

    _____

    (1)

8.  Thomas tells you about his experiences of life as a foreign student. What does he say?

    Good:

    _____

    (1)

    Difficult:

    _____

    (1)

9.  He mentions his experiences of eating in Scotland.

    (a)  What had people warned him about before he left France?

    _____

    (1)

    (b)  What did he discover?

    _____

    (1)

10. Thomas asks whether you would like to go to the local rugby match here at the weekend.

    (a)  Why is it an important match?

    _____

    (1)

(*b*) What does he say about the local rugby team that he supports?

Mention two things.

_____

_____

(2)

11. Thomas explains that there is quite a number of foreign players in French rugby at present.

(*a*) What is good about this?

_____

(1)

(*b*) Explain what the problem is. Mention any one thing.

_____

(1)

12. Thomas explains a **problem** which often arises in some rugby clubs.

(*a*) What is this problem?

_____

_____

(1)

(*b*) What are the clubs doing about it?

_____

(1)

**(25)**

[End of question paper]

_____

_____



_____



_____



_____

_____



_____

(1)

(25)

[End of question paper]

Exam C

# French

# Standard Grade: Credit

Practice Papers
For SQA Exams

Time allowed:
1 hour

**Exam C**
**Credit Level**
**Reading**

**Fill in these boxes:**

Name of centre

Town

Forename(s)

Surname

Make sure you read the questions carefully.

You have 1 hour to complete this paper.

Try to answer all of the questions in the time allowed. Remember to answer in English.

Write your answers in the spaces provided.

Make sure you write as neatly as you can and answer in sentences wherever possible.

You can use a French dictionary.

1. You come across an article in a French magazine where teenagers discuss their relationships with their parents:

Lorsque j'ai un problème et que j'en discute avec mon père, il ne me prend jamais au sérieux. Ensuite, quand je vais trouver ma mère pour parler de mes ennuis, il se plaint. Je me demande parfois s'il n'est pas un peu jaloux.

Julien, 15 ans

Il y a presque dix-huit mois que mes parents se sont séparés et depuis je ne cesse pas d'avoir des disputes avec ma mère. De plus en plus elle se met en colère au sujet de n'importe quoi, ce qui est vraiment dommage car elle était tellement compréhensive quand j'étais plus jeune. Ce que je trouve triste c'est que j'ai l'impression d'avoir perdu non seulement mon père mais aussi ma meilleure amie.

Suzanne, 16 ans

En règle générale mes parents me comprennent assez bien et me donnent tout ce qu'il me faut. Par exemple, ils viennent de m'acheter un nouvel ordinateur pour que je puisse faire des recherches sur internet si j'ai quelque chose à faire pour l'école.

Marc-Antoine, 16 ans

(a) What happens when Julien tries to discuss a problem with his father?

_____

_____

(1)

(b) Explain the father's reaction when Julien turns to his mother. Mention two things.

_____

_____

(2)

(c) How has Suzanne's relationship with her mother deteriorated since her parents' separation? Mention any two things.

_____

_____

(1)

(d) Why does this sadden Suzanne?

_____

_____

(2)

(e) Marc-Antoine talks about the generosity of his parents. What does he say?

_____

_____

(2)

2. In the same magazine, you find an article about the advantages and disadvantages of the internet.

---

**Les dangers de l'internet**

Il est vrai que la technologie nous apportent des biens et, en ce qui concerne l'internet, il y a plusieurs avantages…D'abord cela nous permet de parler à une personne qui se trouve à l'autre côté du monde. L'internet facilitie aussi la vie journalière énormément, par exemple on peut faire les courses sans quitter la maison en utilisant les services du shopping 'on-line' au lieu de faire la queue tous les samedis au supermarché.

Mais on y voit également des inconvénients: on reçoit moins de courrier personnel et par conséquence il nous manque le contact humain de la vraie communication; et on risque de passer des heures entières devant l'écran à surfer et se perdre dans un monde de réalité virtuelle sans avoir conscience de la perte du temps.

---

(*a*)  What are the advantages of the internet? Mention two things.

_____

_____

(2)

(*b*)  What are the disadvantages? Mention two things.

_____

_____

(2)

3.  Later you go on the internet to catch up with some French news under the *Lifestyles* heading. You come across a short piece about a new restaurant in Marseille:

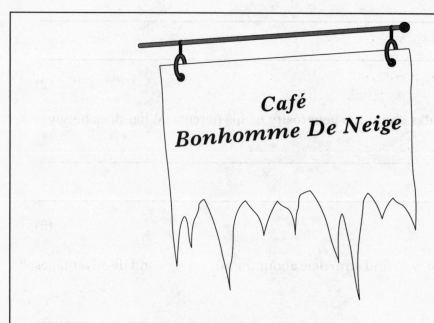

*Café Bonhomme De Neige*

*Pause-café rafraîchissante?*

Un nouveau café est ouvert au centre-ville à Clémenceau, mais c'est un café pas commes les autres, car ici on accueille des clients dans un environnement glacé de –7°C

Conséquence du climat extrême cet hiver en France? Pas du tout! L'intérieur du Café Bonhomme de Neige à Clémenceau est constitué d'une vingtaine de tonnes de glace au total où les gens sont invités à rester pour une durée maximum de trente minutes. Et pour vous qui souffrez d'un léger rhume ou d'un petit mal de gorge, sachez qu'il y a des bénéfices immédiats de cette atmosphère au-dessous de zéro!

(*a*)  How does the café manage to keep the temperature at –7 degrees?

_____

(1)

(b) How does the management prevent the clients from getting too cold?

_____

(1)

(c) What minor ailments are also alleviated by spending a little time here? Mention both things.

_____

(1)

**4.** You read an article about an unusual chain of restaurants in France.

En septembre 1985, Coluche, comique célèbre et véritable icône populaire en France, parle à la radio. Puisque c'est Coluche, tout le monde écoute: il suggère la création des restaurants pour ceux qui n'ont pas de domicile, pour les milliers de 'sans-abris' qui n'ont pas le moyen de préparer ou de se payer un repas chaud.

Peu de temps après, au mois de décembre, ces restaurants, les Restos du Coeur, ouvrent dans les grandes villes, et tout de suite on se rend compte que ce n'est pas seulement les sans-abris qui en ont besoin, mais aussi les pauvres, les chômeurs, les vieux, les malades, les clochards.

Coluche, qui faisait des sketches humoristes et satiriques à la télé est devenu maintenant le sauveur de gens pauvres ou défavorisés.

(a) What was Coluche's idea which was broadcast on French radio in 1985? Mention two things.

_____

_____

(2)

(b) It became clear when the Restos du Coeur opened in December 1985 that many people would benefit from this initiative. Who were they? Mention any two groups.

_____

_____

(2)

(c) How did Coluche's public image change? Mention two things.

_____

_____

(2)

**5.** The success of the Restos du Coeur is celebrated in a special news bulletin.

> Durant la première campagne, en 1985, 5,000 bénévoles ont distribué 8,5 millions de repas.
>
> Aujourd'hui, plus de vingt ans après, 20,000 Restos du Coeur continuent leur mission grâce aux 470,000 donateurs, 41 millions d'euros de dons et de donation par héritage.
>
> En 2008, presque 60,000 bénévoles ont distribué 70 millions de repas, aidé 25,000 bébés de moins de douze mois.
>
> 'Coluche serait fièr de cette réussite', constate la nouvelle directrice des Restos du Coeur. 'Comme il disait au début: <<L'argent ne fait pas le bonheur des pauvres.
>
> Ce qu'on offre aux gens, c'est surtout le contact humain – la pauvreté c'est plus que le manque d'un salaire, c'est aussi l'isolement.>>

(a) Give details of the success of this venture today by completing the sentences. Fill in any three correctly.

20,000 _____ thanks to 470,000 _____

and 41 million Euros _____

In 2008, nearly 60,000 _____ 70 million _____

and helped 25,000 _____

(3)

(b) According to the new director of the company, Coluche understood the needs of poor people. What did he say? Mention two things.

_____

_____

(2)

**(26)**

[End of question paper]

# French

# Standard Grade: Credit

Practice Papers
For SQA Exams

Time allowed:
30 Minutes (Approx)

**Exam C**
**Credit Level**
**Listening Transcript**

The listening transcript accompanies the audio CD provided with the book.

Remember that listening transcripts will **not** be provided when you sit your final exam. They are printed here as an additional item to help you with your revision for the listening exam.

Scotland's leading educational publishers

**Transcript – Credit Level**

**(t)** You are taking part in an exchange visit to France. When you arrive at the train station, you meet your partner, Cédric, and some members of his family.

**(m or f)** **Tu participes à un échange scolaire en France. Quand tu arrives à la gare SNCF, on te présente ton partenaire, Cédric, et quelques membres de sa famille.**

**(t) Question number one**

Cédric explains that his mother is not there to meet you, as she is not well. What does he say about when she fell ill? What exactly is wrong with her? Mention two things.

**(m)** **Samedi dernier on retournait d'une semaine au Maroc et ma mère est tombée malade quand nous sommes arrivés à l'aéroport de Paris. L'après-midi on l'a emmenée à l'hôpital car elle avait de la fièvre et de la diarrhée. Il paraît qu'elle a eu une intoxication alimentaire.**

40 seconds

**(t) Question number two**

You express your hope that it is not serious. What does Cédric's father say to suggest that she is recovering? Mention one thing.

**(m)** **J'espère qu'elle va guérir bientôt. Quand je lui ai rendu visite hier à l'hopital elle avait l'air de retrouver la santé puisqu'elle avait déjà mangé quelque chose à midi.**

40 seconds

**(t) Question number three**

Cédric talks to you about their holiday in Morocco. Why did they go there?

**(m)** **Nous avons passé d'excellentes vacances au Maroc. Mes parents avaient toujours voulu y aller car ma grand-mère est née là-bas et a passé les premières années de sa vie dans le pays.**

40 seconds

**(t) Question number four**

He describes their accommodation. What did he like about its position? Mention two things.

(m) **Nous sommes restés dans une petite maisonnette au centre-ville de Marrakesh, qui donnait sur la place principale. Après avoir mangé le soir on s'amusait à observer la vie nocturne des habitants depuis notre balcon. En plus c'était très commode pour nous parce que ça nous a permis de se reposer un peu l'après-midi quand il faisait trop chaud à l'extérieur.**

40 seconds

(t) **Question number five**

Cédric's father asks you whether you have been elsewhere in France other than Paris. What does he say about the people in Paris. Mention one thing.

(m) **Est-ce que tu as visité d'autres régions en France? Parce que Paris, ce n'est pas la vraie France, tu sais. Comme dans toutes les villes capitales, les gens ici ne s'intéressent qu'à gagner de l'argent et à faire un bénéfice financier des touristes. Ce n'est pas toujours très agréable.**

40 seconds

(t) **Question number six**

He tells you that he grew up in Normandy. What does he say about where he used to live. Mention two things. Why did he have to move to Paris? Mention one thing.

(m) **Moi, je suis normand. Je viens d'un tout petit village en pleine campagne qui s'appelle Canisy, où mon père était instituteur au collège. C'était un petit coin perdu où tout le monde se connaissait et où les voisins faisaient n'importe quoi pour t'aider. Mais, bon, quand j'avais dix-huit ans j'ai dû quitter la maison pour poursuivre mes études à la faculté de droit à Paris et c'est ici où j'ai trouvé mon premier emploi.**

40 seconds

(t) **Question number seven**

You meet Cédric's older sister, Louise, who is home for the weekend. She talks to you about her new job. What exactly does she do? Mention two things. Mention one thing she did last week.

(f) **Je viens de commencer un nouveau poste comme journaliste pour le journal du Nord de la France pour lequel j'écris des articles sur l'environnement et le mouvement écologiste. J'adore mon métier, car la vie de journaliste est très varié mais exigeant à la fois. La semaine dernière, par exemple, j'ai fait une interview avec le maire de Caen, j'ai parlé aux lycéens sur le problème de la pollution, et j'ai écrit un article sur une manifestation d'étudiants à l'université.**

40 seconds

(t) **Question number eight**

Louise tells you how she trained for her job. What does she say? Mention two things. What does she say about the route her boss took?

(f) **J'ai entendu dire qu'il n'est pas nécessaire d'aller à l'université pour devenir journaliste. C'est vrai, mais moi, je voulais bien étudier et j'ai fait ma formation de journalisme à l'universite pendant trois** ans et après j'ai fait un stage professionnel chez un magazine pour les adolescents. Par contre, mon patron n'a jamais fait d'études universitaires – il a eu son premier poste pour une station de radio quelques mois après son baccalauréat.

40 seconds

**(t) Question number nine**

Cédric talks about his own future plans. Give details of what he would like to do.

**(m) Ce que j'aimerais faire, moi, c'est de travailler comme moniteur de ski en hiver et donner des cours d'escalade dans une école d'alpinisme en été. J'ai toujours adoré les activités sportives à la montagne et mon rêve c'est de gagner ma vie à faire quelque chose qui m'intéresse.**

40 seconds

**(t) Question number ten**

Cédric's father comes in with news about his mother. What does the hospital expect to happen? Mention one thing. What symptoms does she no longer have?

**(m) J'ai reçu un coup de téléphone de l'hôpital. D'après le médecin, ça va beaucoup mieux maintenant avec ta mère et il souhaite qu'elle sorte de l'hôpital soit demain ou le lendemain matin. Elle n'a plus mal au ventre ni mal à la tête.**

40 seconds

**(t) Question number eleven**

His father asks whether you and Cédric would mind picking up something in town. What is it he wishes you to get? What might be the problem?

**(m) Si vous aviez le temps, vous deux, je serais très reconnaissant si vous pouviez aller à la pharmacie pour les médicaments pour maman. Tenez, je vous donne l'ordonnance. Mais vous devez vous dépêcher un peu parce que demain c'est un jour férié et les magasins vont fermer aujourd'hui de bonne heure.**

40 seconds

**(t) Question number twelve**

Cédric's father tells you of his plans for this evening. What arrangements has he made for this evening? Why does he think it would be a good idea to invite along Gerard?

**(m) Alors ce soir, nous avons prévu de faire un barbecue sur la terrasse vers huit heures si le beau temps continue. Cédric, tu peux inviter ton ami, Gérard, si tu voulais. Ce serait intéressant pour ton partenaire de faire sa connaissance – il sait bien parler l'anglais et lui aussi participe à l'échange. Qu'en penses-tu?**

40 seconds

[End of transcript]

# French

# Standard Grade: Credit

| | | |
|---|---|---|
| Practice Papers<br>For SQA Exams | Time allowed:<br>30 Minutes (approx) | **Exam C**<br>**Credit Level**<br>**Listening** |

**Fill in these boxes:**

Name of centre

Town

Forename(s)

Surname

The listening exam should take approximately 30 minutes.

You will hear a number of items in French. These items are repeated three times.

There will then be a pause to let you write your answer. Make sure you read the questions carefully.

Remember to answer in English and write your answers in the spaces provided.

You cannot use a French dictionary.

Scotland's leading educational publishers

You are taking part in an exchange visit to France. When you arrive at the train station, you meet your partner, Cédric, and some members of his family.

Tu participes à un échange scolaire en France. Quand tu arrives à la gare SNCF, on te présente ton partenaire, Cédric, et quelques membres de sa famille.

1. Cédric explains that his mother is not there to meet you, as she is not well.

   (a) What does he say about **when** she fell ill?

   _____

   (1)

   (b) What exactly was wrong with her? Mention two things.

   _____

   _____

   (2)

2. What does Cédric's father say to suggest that she is recovering? Mention one thing.

   _____

   (1)

3. Cédric talks to you about their holiday in Morocco. Why did they go there? Mention any one thing.

   _____

   (1)

4. He describes their accommodation. What did he like about its position? Mention any two things.

   _____

   _____

   (2)

5. Cédric's father asks you whether you have been elsewhere in France other than Paris. What does he say about the people in Paris? Mention any one thing.

   _____

   (1)

**6.** He tells you that he grew up in Normandy.

    (*a*)  What does he say about where he used to live? Mention two things.

        _____

        _____

                                                          (2)

    (*b*)  Why did he have to move to Paris?

        _____

                                                          (1)

**7.** You meet Cédric's older sister, Louise, who is home for the weekend. She talks to you about her new job.

    (*a*)  What exactly does she do? Mention any one thing.

        _____

        _____

                                                          (1)

    (*b*)  What did she do last week? Mention any one thing.

        _____

                                                          (1)

**8.** Louise tells you how she trained for her job.

    (*a*)  What does she say? Mention two things.

        _____

        _____

                                                          (2)

    (*b*)  What does she say about the route her boss took?

        _____

        _____

                                                          (1)

**9.** Cédric talks about his own future plans. What would he like to do? Mention two things.

_____

_____

(2)

**10.** Cédric's father comes in with news about his mother.

What does he say? Mention two things.

_____

_____

(2)

**11.** His father asks whether you and Cédric would mind picking up something in town.

(a) What is it?

_____

(1)

(b) What might be the problem? Mention any one thing.

_____

(1)

**12.** Cédric's father talks about his plans for that evening.

(a) What arrangement has he made?

_____

(1)

(b) Why does he think it would be a good idea to invite Gérard? Mention two things.

_____

_____

(2)

**25**

[End of question paper]

Worked Answers

**READING EXAM A**                                 **WORKED ANSWERS**

**NOTE :**
- **it is impossible to account for all correct versions of the answer; it is essential, therefore, for markers to be satisfied that the main point is communicated in terms of accuracy and spirit**
- **something in brackets is not necessary**
- **something underlined is necessary**
- **if an extra detail or answer is given (e.g. 3 details are given by the candidate when just 2 are requested, then the extra detail must not show misunderstanding or a critical error or contradict a correct answer; if it does, then a point should be deducted)**
- **warnings regarding some common errors are given on occasions below**
- **in general, all the details in the answer scheme are required**

## Question 1

> Questions 1–3 are a good example of how a single topic or theme might stretch over a number of questions – here the French film 'Entre les murs' occupies not only 1–3 but also 12/26 points of the Credit Reading paper. This means that it is very important for candidates to ensure a good understanding of the opening question and also to work hard at the links between all three questions on the subject.

(a)  You need (firstly) to captivate them / get their interest/attention      (1)

You need to have a close / honest / direct relationship with the pupils      (1)

**2**

*HINT* > The importance of understanding the opening question by the magazine's interviewer needs to be emphasised, as it helps you with the answer: here the slightly unusual 'Quel enseignant est François?' is used instead of an easier version, such as 'Il est comment comme professeur, François?' or 'Il est quel genre de professeur, François?', in order to test the reader's ability to cope with difficult or advanced question forms. It really is worth revising these!

(b)  He loves discussing (things) with pupils / he knows how to have a dialogue with them

OR

he knows it / teaching is about more than (imparting) knowledge      **1**

(c)  They are actors (***not*** comedians)      (1)

They are used to improvising      (1)

**2**

**TOP EXAM TIP**

Beware the inclusion of the *faux ami* or 'false friend': of course, *comédien* does not mean 'comedian', it means 'actor'!

## Question 2

(a)   it is a documentary fiction / part documentary, part fiction           (1)

   it shows what really happens in a real school                          (1)

                                                                          **2**

(b)   he told them to talk normally / not to change how they normally talk   (1)

| HINT | One of the challenging aspects here is the change of tenses – from *imperfect (past)*, telling what the director found of interest at the outset of filming, to the *present*, where he is explaining and describing what *normally* happens in a real school, to the *perfect (past)*, when he talks of how the pupils did the scenes and created the characters. |

## Question 3

> It is important here to try to build up an image in your mind's eye of the kind of school the collège Dalto is. This is an essential factor in comprehension, both in reading and listening.

(a)   because there was a geographical <u>and</u> social mix / people were from different geographical <u>and</u> social backgrounds                                (1)

(b)   There were (about) 40 (different) nationalities                          (1)
   (some) pupils were at the bottom of the social scale/lower end of society (1)

                                                                          **2**

## Question 4

> One of the difficult things to get used to is the switching from one topic to another – the only thing that connects question 4 to what has preceded is the internet! And don't worry – no one is expecting you to be an expert on rare diseases. It is not a test of your scientific knowledge, but rather of your ability to piece together a little story or narrative from the short extract.

(a)   he made an emergency landing                                           (1)

(b)   Any 3:

   he felt ill <u>during the night</u>

   he had a (high) temperature/ fever

   <u>he complained</u> of dizziness

   he fell unconscious                                                     (3)

(c) <u>voluntary</u> work in the Congo / Africa                                    (1)

    (***not*** he was with his fiancée or some EC students, etc.)

    in an orphanage                                                          (1)

> **HINT**    Caution! Not **whom** he had been with but rather **what** he had been doing *there*!

## Question 5

 Credit Reading often involves facts, figures and statistics, particularly when an important development in the numbers of something has occurred. Special attention would have to be paid normally to written numbers *mille (1000)*, *million (1000 000)* and *milliard (1000,000,000)*!

A stock of vocabulary including tricky numbers, dates and words such as *chiffre (number) croissance (increase), décroissance, dimunition, (both decrease), nombreux (many/numerous)* etc., are an obvious asset to understanding this kind of database literature.

(a) International Day of Rare Diseases                                        (1)

(b) there are <u>more than</u> 5,500                                           (1)

    this number is always changing                                       (1)

                                            **2**

(c) that 2 new rare diseases...                                              (1)

    described in it / discovered <u>every month</u>                         (1)

                                     **2**

> **TOP EXAM TIP**
>
> Be mindful not to add to what is said in the text. Remember that this is not a general test of your biology, but of your comprehension of precisely what is said, so resist the temptation to add anything extra that you might know of the subject, as it could lose you marks.

(d) when it affects (less than) 1 person in (every) 200/

    (less than) 30,000 in a country such as France          **1**

## Question 6

 Throughout the General and Credit papers there are questions that test your ability to cope with arrangements – mainly social, like this one, or group/organisation arrangements, where something like a school exchange is involved.

(a) Any 2:

    boat trips

    (long) walks/walking

    archery                                                                  **2**

> **HINT**    Again, mention all 3 to be safe.

(b)  because he is going to <u>Germany on a school exchange</u> /
   because he'll only be at home until Friday night          (1)

**(26)**

> **TOP EXAM TIP**
>
> It is important here to explain fully –
> marks will not generally be given out
> at Credit for single facts (such as 'he
> is going to Germany') when they are
> not backed up with exemplification of
> some kind.

---

## LISTENING EXAM A                          WORKED ANSWERS

### Question 1

>
> The *flashback* is used regularly at credit level to test candidates' ability to
> understand the perfect tense, and generally to switch from the present
> scene to a previous. *Tense awareness* is a vital part of your comprehension
> skills, and too often revision for listening centres exclusively on learning
> vocabulary rather than the crucial revision of tenses.

Any 2 :

– she was born in Tunisia where she lived for her first <u>11 years</u>
  (*not* until she was 11)                                      (1)

– mother worked (there) as a doctor <u>in the hospital in Tunis/in the capital</u>   (1)

– father worked in the <u>French</u> (high) <u>school</u>

– (*not* worked as a French teacher)                           (1)

**2**

> **HINT** ⟩ Remember to include full details, about where exactly she lived and for how long, the
> precise nature of her parents' jobs, etc.

### Question 2

Any one :

– they are twins                                               (1)

– they are *three years* younger than her                      (1)

**1**

> **HINT** ⟩ The clue for one of the details lies in the fact that the sisters are the same age!

## Question 3

 We now switch to the *imperfect*, as Clémentine begins to reminisce about the *way things were generally*.

Any 2 :

— she missed the North African climate (1)

— she found it difficult to make friends at school/where she lived (1)

— she didn't know anybody at school from her area **2**

**TOP EXAM TIP**

Remember to include the *reason* in your answer!

## Question 4

(a) the geographical diversity/variety/range (a clumsy expression of this might be accepted, but the point about the different geography within France needs to be clear)/ the forests and coastlines (1)

(b) (being members of) the regional gymnastics team (1)

**2**

 **HINT**  It is important to mention what aspect of life in France she appreciated rather than just mention 1 type of holiday location she enjoyed – remember that the locations given are only examples of the general point the examiners are seeking.

**HINT**  Again, full details of their involvement in the sport are required. You would not get a point at credit for the translation of the simple sport itself!

## Question 5

 You are now listening about Clémentine's sister, rather than Clémentine herself, and to complicate matters further, she moves from the perfect tense to the present. Common sense should help you make the link between what the sister has done and what she can do now as a result!

— she improved/perfected her English OR she speaks English really well/ fluently (1)

— she matured / is more adult now (1)

**2**

**Question 6**

> This is a good example of using another family member's experiences to discuss something of general interest, such as the eating habits of Americans. You have to be ready to go with the flow!

(a) They go 2-3 times a week to fast food restaurants OR they have breakfast at the fast food restaurant (1)

(b) they have health problems *later on* (in life) OR they *have become* obese (1)

**2**

**Question 7**

> The inevitable *compare and contrast* between eating habits in Scotland and France has arrived!

(a) Scots eat <u>more</u> sweet things (1)

Scots eat <u>more</u> fatty/greasy foods/a lot of fatty food compared with French (1)

(b) the differences in eating/cooking habits are exaggerated

OR

The Scots have made some progress/got better/improved (1)

**3**

**Question 8**

> This question is worth 2 points, so 1 point will be awarded for every 2 correct gap-filling. 2 correct gap-fillings = 1 point; all 4 = 2 points
>
> Also, listen out for the comparison, of last year and now, signalled by the but below!

Every Friday <u>she goes to the gym</u>

but <u>that kind of physical exercise is really boring/painful</u>

Now <u>they eat a balanced/varied diet well/healthily</u>

and in the evening <u>she (and her mother) take(s) the dog for a walk</u>  **2**

**Question 9**

> There is rarely a mention of a parent without a discussion of the relationship with the child! And in such cases, be ready for the *good vs bad in the relationship!*

(a)  her mother treats her as/like an adult          (1)

(b)  that she needs a bit more freedom               (1)

**2**

## Question 10

(a)  (foreign/modern) languages                      (1)

(b)  she will find a/her own flat (in town) OR she will be/ become more independent          (1)

> **TOP EXAM TIP**
>
> Careful here – there are 3 details in the French., so it is unlikely that 1 point will be awarded for a single detail only!

**2**

## Question 11

> Common sense could help you with this one – why wouldn't someone want to become a teacher? (Mmm... let me think...)

> **TOP EXAM TIP**
>
> Don't fall into the trap of too-brief answers, such as 'preparation', 'marking' 'meetings' etc., It's the details of these we're after!

Any 3 :

– it is very demanding/exacting
   (**not** hard/difficult/stressful)               (1)

– you have to put in <u>extra/additional/supplementary</u> hours          (1)

– preparing <u>lessons</u>                          (1)

– marking/correcting                                (1)

– extra-curricular activities                       (1)

– meetings                                          (1)

**3**

## Question 12

– being useful OR helping others                    (1)

> **TOP EXAM TIP**
>
> No points will be given for saying what she *doesn't* think is important! Also, mention only one if in doubt about the meaning of the second detail, otherwise you could cancel out the correct answer with an error.

## Question 13

> No credit listening would be complete without an arrangement of some kind – this time mixed in with some hi-tech language! You might find it useful to list the topics covered in this paper, and jot down the examples of the tenses under separate columns. This will remind you of how much breadth and depth there is in this paper.

– she will give you her mobile phone number         (1)

**(25)**

## READING EXAM B                                      WORKED ANSWERS

**NOTE :**

- it is impossible to account for all correct versions of the answer; it is essential, therefore, for markers to be satisfied that the main point is communicated in terms of accuracy and spirit
- something in brackets is not necessary
- something underlined is necessary
- if an extra detail or answer is given (e.g. 3 details are given by the candidate when just 2 are requested, then the extra detail must not show misunderstanding or a critical error or contradict a correct answer; if it does, then a point should be deducted)
- warnings regarding some common errors are given on occasions below
- in general, all the details in the answer scheme are required

### Question 1

 Although the individual texts are short, this article is quite demanding, as it requires the reader to understand what physical demands are made of the sports mentioned and how these sports have become popular as a result. In other words, you are being tested on your ability to grasp the *processes* by which the sports are performed and enjoyed. Clearly, the *use of verbs* is the main area of focus in this.

Swimming is a complete sport where
<u>all the muscles have to work/be used without risk of injury</u>                    (1)

Handicapped children benefit from swimming because
<u>it allows them to/they can exercise on their own/</u>
<u>do it alone in the presence of a life-guard</u>                    (1)

Horse-riding will not strain your muscles provided that
<u>you don't lose /you keep your balance</u>                    (1)

When riding you have the opportunity to
<u>work in harmony with the animal while (benefiting from) being outside</u>  (1)

Football encourages
<u>(good) relations/getting on with others</u>                    (1)

                                                            **(5)**

**TOP EXAM TIP**

It is essential to explain and describe in good English but at the same time ensure that all the features of the original French are included each time

## Question 2

Not for the first time, the *importance of questions in an interview* is raised, and your ability to work out what is being asked will not only determine your award for question 2 a), but will also affect your comprehension of Chabal's answers!

(*a*)  are you still hungry/really wanting to play (beneath the blue/ French jersey)                                                                1

(*b*)  there is a good atmosphere (in Scotland)                          (1)
they/the Scots play with passion                                          (1)
                                                                         2

> **HINT**  The use of *on* can be confusing in French, as it depends on which person or group has already been referred to. Here *on* refers to *les Ecossais*, not the French!

(*c*)  **any 2 from 3** :

representing his country
doing his best
it is a team game rather than an individual one                          (2)
                                                                         2

> **HINT**  Sometimes it's the obvious answer they're looking for, such as an international rugby player wanting to *represent his country!* Also, be sure to explain *fully* that 'it is a *team* game' as opposed to an *individual* sport – again, state the obvious!

(*d*)  it is (like being in) one big family                                1

## Question 3

Whether or not it genuinely interests young people of your age, Credit pupils can always expect a question relating to the environment. There is a real commitment to test candidates' ability to cope with wider or more global issues at this level.

(*a*)  to find out/research into what is being done in Normandy/locally/in the region to protect nature/the environment                              1

(*b*)  ministers <u>and</u> manufacturing industries/manufacturers        1

(*c*)  any 2 from 3 :

those that are not tested on animals                                      (1)
those that are not harmful to the environment/do not have chemicals
that are harmful to the environment                                       (1)
                                                                         2

> **HINT** The main difficulty with a question like this is in identifying where exactly in the text the answer to any one question lies. A useful tip is to underline or highlight the relevant part of the text each time.

(d) (the construction of) new hypermarkets/ Supermarkets/factories **1**

> **TOP EXAM TIP**
> Be sure to avoid abbreviating the original French: facts relating to both the animals and chemicals are needed in your response.

(e) they were protected/conservation areas **1**

## Question 4

 This is an example of one of the most common formats of Credit Reading, whereby you are given diverse opinions of a single issue. It is amazing how much some common-sense thinking can contribute to your understanding here, so spend a moment brainstorming the likely points of view first!

(a) any 1 from 2 :

the different teaching/ learning styles

group activities _instead of_

working individually **1**

(b) didn't share his interests/hobbies (1)

his partner was interested _only_ in playing on his computer (1)

**2**

(c) any 3 from 5 :

in Scotland they _rarely ate/eat together_ (1)

everyone helped themselves / took what they wanted (1)

they snacked/nibbled sweets/sweet things _in between meals_ (1)

they ate what they wanted

their diet isn't good for health **3**

> **TOP EXAM TIP**
> Points will be dropped if any of the details in the French are omitted – this kind of omission _costs many candidates a Credit award._

(d) the family did everything they could to make her feel at ease/at home (1)

they gave her an excellent memory/experience of the country (1)

**2**

(e) invitation to go over for _2 weeks this summer_ (1)

and (perhaps) visit the _grandparents who live in the northwest_ (1)

**2**

> **HINT** Again, you don't know for sure what the marks will be awarded for here, so _every detail of the summer holiday in France_ should be mentioned.

**(26)**

| LISTENING EXAM B | WORKED ANSWERS |
|---|---|

## Question 1

 Social arrangements are a common theme at this level, often involving time and potential problems.

– On Thursdays there are always lots of people there/it is always busy (1)

– If you arrive after 5 p.m., it is /you will find it difficult to find a court (1)

**2**

## Question 2

 This question focuses on the comparison of what happens normally with the events of this period at present.

– Normally, he is not allowed to go out during the week (1)

– But at present, (he is allowed to because) it is the end of term / the Scottish pupils are over here / he can out with the Scottish pupils (1)

**2**

HINT You must learn to use the information you are already given about the setting to assist with the answers: you know, for example, that this paper involves a school exchange, so you need to apply some common sense and imagine how this would change the normal routine of host families, such as that of Bazire.

## Question 3

 Complex relationships with parents, nearly always giving good and bad points, often feature at this level.

HINT Be careful to be *specific* about the nature of this year at school. Marks will not be given for vague replies, such as 'this is an important year at school', even if they are correct in spirit.

– he has lots of homework this year/as it is a busy year at school (***not*** an important year) (1)

– it is not (always) safe in some areas in town (1)

**2**

## Question 4

(a) his father is over protective / he does not let him do things on his own  (1)

(b) about (his) freedom/independence  (1)

**2**

>
> **HINT** Again, don't be tempted to make a general comment about his relationship with both parents, such as 'he gets on well with them both', as you are being asked _specifically about his father_ here.

## Question 5

> ★ More arrangements to get to grips with! This is a recurring theme in this paper!

(a) they would like to go camping in the mountains / near the Spanish border  (1)

(**no points** for repeating the information given in the question about his going on holiday with school friends)

> **HINT** It is important to give fullest possible details here, even though only one point is awarded – don't gamble with the marking scheme

(b) she thinks he should stay at home/ she thinks he is too young (to go on holiday without his parents)  (1)

**2**

>
> **HINT** You are being asked to work out the complexity of the timing/order of events that Bazire's mother is concerned with here – it is not just the need for a holiday job, but _when_ that should be that's important.

## Question 6

> ★ This is a good example of a question where the text moves on quickly from one set of details (about the job) to another (about what discipline Bazire will find hard) without any warning...

(a) 1 from 3 :

– he would work in a little <u>North African</u> restaurant (in the town centre) on a Friday and Saturday

– and would work in the kitchen <u>of a restaurant</u>

– and clear the tables (at the end of the night) <u>in a restaurant</u>  (1)

> **TOP EXAM TIP**
> Fullest details, please! You don't know exactly what they're after, so give it all!

    (*b*)  he would find it difficult to save his money / not to spend it (immediately)

                                                                                          (1)

                                                                                                **3**

## Question 7

> Beware the introduction of a new character midway through the listening paper – this always means a completely new direction of the narrative!

    (*a*)  he was a student/studying/part of a student group at the university
          (of St. Andrews)                                                 (1)

> **HINT**    The mention of proper nouns, such as St. Andrews and Erasmus, can be distracting. In fact, they are not essential to the answer at all, and should be taken as the mere *setting.*

    (*b*)  he was able to study Scottish history <u>and</u> play golf             (1)

                                                                                                          **2**

## Question 8

    –  good = everyone was /people were/they were extremely nice/kind    (1)

    –  difficult = accent hard to understand/people spoke fast <u>in shops and pubs</u> OR
        it wasn't exactly the kind of English they had learnt at school    (1)

                                                                                                    **2**

> **HINT**    You are being tested on your ability to understand *exactly where or when* the difficulties arose, so avoid vague replies, like 'he couldn't understand the accent'. Again, it's correct, but *not worthy of credit* !

## Question 9

> Cultural comparisons are common at this level, so a well prepared candidate will have thought about which topics involve such comparisons of lifestyle – eating habits, education, free time all spring to mind.

    (*a*)  that the food in Scotland would be bad/unhealthy/greasy/fatty    (1)

> **HINT**    This is a pure test of key topic vocabulary, so *specific details* are required!

    (*b*)  he ate very well <u>in the canteen</u> OR (he was surprised by) the quality of the
        food in the student
        <u>refectory/canteen</u>                                                               (1)

**Question 10**

(a) it is the semi-final of the (regional) cup                                    (1)

(b) it is very good/strong (at present)                                          (1)

two members have been selected to play for the national team/France    (1)

**3**

**Question 11**

 The mention of the _nationalities_ is not particularly significant compared with the notion of foreign players.

HINT > Specifically, this tests your understanding of 'plus passionnant' and 'rémunérés' and 'augmenté'. This emphasises once more the need to learn the more advanced vocabulary of the course, especially given that there is no dictionary allowed in this paper.

(a) it makes the sport more spectacular/exciting (for everyone/to watch)    (1)

(b) one from two :
these players/the foreign players/the English/Australian/New Zealand players earn a lot_/ are well paid
the tickets are much more expensive (than before)
(the link must be made between the high earning and the price of the tickets)
(1)

**2**

**Question 12**

(a) (lots of) players don't speak good French                                  (1)

(b) they make them go to French lessons/classes                              (1)

HINT > Do not be distracted by the word 'vedette' – what is important here is the _idea_ of the foreign players having to learn French/go back to the classroom, not that they are stars.

**(25)**

**TOP EXAM TIP**

Have you thought through how you can benefit from the 5 minutes at the end of the listening paper? Might it encourage you to transcribe or make notes during the listening if you knew you had the time to return to these scribbles at the end? How can you usefully fill in the time given? Can extra points be gained?

## READING EXAM C                    WORKED ANSWERS

**NOTE :**

- it is impossible to account for all correct versions of the answer; it is essential, therefore, for markers to be satisfied that the main point is communicated in terms of accuracy and spirit
- something in brackets is not necessary
- something underlined is necessary
- if an extra detail or answer is given (e.g. 3 details are given by the candidate when just 2 are requested, then the extra detail must not show misunderstanding or a critical error or contradict a correct answer; if it does, then a point should be deducted)
- warnings regarding some common errors are given on occasions below
- in general, all the details in the answer scheme are required

**Question 1**

> *Family relationships* is a common topic in Credit Reading, as it requires the ability of the candidate to understand both the general issues and the specific examples of problems at home, particularly where there is a contrast – whether that be in good versus bad qualities, or the relationship with one parent versus the other, or the difference between past and present. The roles of *comparisons, descriptive adjectives and past and present tenses* are therefore of special importance here.

**TOP EXAM TIP**

Remember: *Read the introduction and questions in English first,* before you scan the French texts, as these will give you a summary of the main issues of what the three teenagers say in advance of reading their accounts.

(a)  – he never takes him/it seriously                                    **1**

(b)  – he complains                                                        (1)

     – he becomes (a little) jealous (of her/the mother)                   (1)

                                                                           **2**

**HINT** > You are being tested on how well you have understood not only the relationship between Julien and his father but also the implied relationship between father and mother.

(c)  **any 2 :**

     – she <u>constantly/all the time</u> argues with her mother

     – her mother gets angry <u>about nothing at all/everything</u>

     – her mother used to be understanding (but not now)

                                                                           **2**

(d)  she feels that she has not only lost a/her father <u>but also her best friend</u>

                                                                           **1**

(e)  – they bought him a (new) computer                                    (1)

     – so that he could (go on the internet) do work/research for school   (1)

                                                                           **2**

**Question 2**

Questions on information technology have been part of Credit Reading for a good 10 years now, and we have got to the stage where *the dangers or disadavantages of computers* is a popular theme, so it makes sense to revise your *checklist of pros and cons of computers,* such that you are familiar with these points in advance of the testing.

(*a*) any 2 :

    – we/you can speak to someone <u>at the other side of the world</u>     (1)

    – you can shop on line (which makes everyday life easier)/

    – you can save the hours queuing at the supermarket     (1)

2

(*b*) – you don't get as much personal mail / you lose out on human contact or real communication     (1)

    – you risk spending hours in front of the computer screen / losing yourself <u>in a world of virtual reality</u>     (1)

2

**Question 3**

From the predictable to the bizarre! The key here is to try to *visualise the café!* On a serious note, it is important to expose yourself to as many unusual short texts as you can, as Credit Reading is a *test of your strength to cope with some off-the-wall articles* and get some credit for it, as there will be many who are sitting this level of the exam who will simply throw in the towel at this prospect!

(*a*) – (around) 20 tonnes of ice in the café/the café is made out of 20 tonnes of ice

      [key is the idea that the cafe is made out of ice]     1

(*b*) – there is a limit of 30 minutes / you can spend a maximum of 30 minutes

1

(*c*) – a <u>slight</u> cold <u>and</u> a sore throat

1

## Question 4

 Here is an example of the question appearing to be about a celebrity (Coluche), whereas it in fact is about the wider, more important issues that celebrity got involved in.

(a) restaurants for the homeless... (1)

... don't have the means/can't afford to make / buy (themselves) a hot meal (1)

OR restaurants for people who can't afford a hot meal = 2 points

**2**

(b) any 4 (1 point per 2 mention; if only 3 mentioned, 1 point awarded)
the poor/unemployed/elderly/sick/tramps or down-and-outs **2**

**HINT** > Be careful here to mention *the full list* – you cannot afford to try to calculate just how marks will be awarded, so include all 6 groups in the text. Is your dictionary up to this task? If not, be thinking about the consequence of that!

(c) he/Coluche has gone from <u>satirical</u> comedian in provocative TV sketches... (1)

...to (the) saviour of the underprivileged/poor (or equivalent) (1)

**2**

**HINT** > This is getting *close to translation* at Credit level (which people normally associate with Higher): the markers are looking for your ability to convey the subtle conversion of Coluche from one type of public figure to another, and are also interested in your wording in English of such phrases as 'économiquement faibles'.

## Question 5

 Another instance of the continuing story, as the Coluche narrative carries into the next question. Important here is to retain what you have gathered from question 4 about the whole initiative of the Restos du Coeur. The inclusion of a data-based question, with facts and figures is commonplace at this level, and is surprisingly testing. It's not the numbers that are difficult; it's what they relate to!

(a) any 3 from 6 :

- 20,000 Restos du Coeur continue the mission

- thanks to 47,000 <u>donors</u> and

- 41 million Euros <u>from donations/donors and bequests/ left in people's wills.</u>

- In 2008, nearly 60,000 <u>volunteers distributed</u>

- 70 million <u>meals</u>

- and <u>helped 25,000 babies under (the age of) 12 months</u>

**TOP EXAM TIP**

Make sure that the whole re-written paragraph makes sense in English, as well as giving the information of the French text.

**3**

(b)  money doesn't make the poor happy                                             (1)

poverty is about more than what you earn / poverty is (also) about feeling
isolated/lonely                                                                    (1)

**(26)**

## LISTENING EXAM C                                          WORKED ANSWERS

### Question 1

> The situation of an exchange is frequently used to tie together various scenes, so you will need to be prepared to switch your attention from one topic to another quickly. This is the main reason why the learning of topic-based vocabulary is so important at Standard Grade. It is worth, for example, making a list of all the different topics from your syllabus that are covered here, so that this point is fully appreciated.

(a)  she fell ill while returning from holiday/ Morocco
/when they arrived at the airport                                (1)

(b)  she had a temperature                                        (1)

she had diarrhea                                                  (1)

**3**

> **TOP EXAM TIP**
>
> It is vital that you grasp the situation or scene that is set right away, as a failure to do this may result in confusion over a number of questions. Try to visualise the scene of the family returning home from holiday...

### Question 2

she had already eaten/had something to eat yesterday (when he visited)          **1**

> **HINT**   Your ability to cope with timescale is tested here, as questions 3, 4 and 5 refer to things that have already happened, but not necessarily in chronological order. Note the use of the pluperfect *had already eaten* here.

### Question 3

any one from :

because his parents <u>had always wanted </u>to go there
because his grandmother was born there
because his grandmother grew up there                                          **1**

> **HINT**   Note the use of the pluperfect *had always wanted* here.

### Question 4

any 2 :

the bedroom looked out on to the main/high street

they could watch the night life (after dinner/from their balcony) they could watch passers-by/people go by

they were able to (go back and) rest/escape the heat <u>in the afternoons</u>    **2**

**HINT**  What is important here is that you identify the advantages of their accommodation at the *various times of day.*

## Question 5

  The subject of their holiday is being left behind as the attention turns to your own experiences in France. Questions 5 and 6 focus on opinions of places and people there.

they are interested only in <u>making/earning</u> money/

they want to make a profit/money from tourists

(***not*** they are/it is unpleasant)    **1**

## Question 6

You are expected to follow the change in tense from *present*, in question 5, to *imperfect* in question 6 where, typically for this tense, *the ways things were* is being described.

(*a*)  any 2 :

he used to live/ grew up in a little village <u>in the country</u>
everyone knew one another

(***not*** his father was a teacher there)    (2)

(*b*)  to study/go to university / to find his first job    (1)

                                                            **3**

## Question 7

Again, your ability to follow the characters involved and the subsequent switch of speaker, tense and situation, is all tested at once!

(*a*)  any one from :

she is a journalist with / she works for a regional/local/North of France newspaper

she writes articles on the environment    (1)

**HINT**  Full details should be noted here – *do not gamble* with what the answer scheme requires!

(b)  any one from :

she spoke to (high) school children/pupils/students <u>about the pollution</u> (problem)

she interviewed Caen's Mayor    (1)

2

> **TOP EXAM TIP**
>
> Be prepared to mention all relevant details of at least two things to be safe. Marks at this level will not be awarded for simply stating, for instance, 'she interviewed someone', or 'she discussed the pollution problems', etc.

## Question 8

(a)  any one from :

she studied /trained in <u>journalism</u> <u>at university</u> (for 3 years)    (1)

she did a placement/work experience/stint with a <u>teenage magazine</u>    (1)

> HINT   The word 'trained' may make you a little uncertain, so best mention her entire studies and work experience prior to getting this job.

(b)  any one from :

he left school after his baccalaureate/he didn't go to university

he worked for a radio station    (1)

3

## Question 9

> From the sister's past to Cédric's future – another switch of person and tense!

he would like to be a ski <u>instructor/monitor/teacher</u> (in the winter)    (1)

he would like to <u>work/teach</u> in a climbing school (in summer)    (1)

(in both cases, the idea of teaching rather than just taking part in the activity is essential)

> HINT   Be sure to include seasons!

## Question 10

> This is why it is necessary to grasp the situation described in questions 1 and 2 – Credit Listening often forces the candidate to return to the scene set earlier on in the paper!
>
> There is always one problem or another described at this level, and if that subject is something like illness, then you are required to give full details not only of the condition but also of the arrangements involved.

she is <u>a lot</u> better

they expect his mother to be released from hospital <u>tomorrow morning</u>

2

## Question 11

> There is occasionally an assumption that candidates know something of the French way of life, and here an understanding of the many short holidays, or *jours fériés*, in France, and of the opening and closing of shops in such periods, is useful ! So the culture of the country as well as the language, can be a feature.

(a)   medicine <u>for the mother</u>                                                                                       (1)

(b)   any 2 from 3 :

    you'll have to be there early

    the shops will be shutting <u>early</u>

    it's a (an annual) holiday/festival/fête tomorrow                                        (1)

                                                                                                                                    **2**

## Question 12

> Remember the original setting – you are on an exchange visit to France!

(a)   a barbecue <u>on the terrace</u> /at (around) <u>8 o'clock</u> /<u>if the good weather continues</u>                                        (1)

> **HINT**   Be mindful of the importance of the word *parler*.

**TOP EXAM TIP**

A final test of your grasp of arrangements – remember to include all details of the evening planned.

(b)   because Gérard is taking part in the exchange                                        (1)

    he can bring his (exchange) partner                                                            (1)

                                                                                                                                    **3**

                                                                                                                                 **(25)**

> **HINT**   Ensure that you spend the 5 -minute check over the paper to good effect. It may well be that you have had to transcribe the actual French word or phrase during the listening because you could not put it into English at the time. This period at the end of the paper gives you the chance to go over such notes and make sure that no blanks are left at any stage.